C000297284

David Young 1940 RAF Scampton.

My Long March Home

To the Angel on my shoulder

Alan Young
Pat Young McEwan

Merlin Massara Publishing

Merlin Massara Publishing

Copyright © 2012 Alan Young

The right of Alan Young and Pat Young McEwan to be identified as the Authors of the Work has been
asserted by them in accordance with the Copyright, Design and Patents Act 1988

First published in Great Britain by Merlin Massara Publishing in 2012
All rights reserved. No part of this publication may be reproduced, stored in a retrieval system, or
transmitted in any form or by other means without the written permission of the publishers, nor be
otherwise circulated in any form of binding, cover or sleeve other than that in which it is published and
without similar conditions being imposed on the subsequent purchaser

ISBN 9780954390037

The Author and Publishers have made all reasonable efforts to clarify ownership
of any quoted content or copyright and have acknowledged accordingly.
However, if errors have been unintentionally made, owners are invited to contact
the publishers so that acknowledgement can be given.

Production management by Holly Noonan
Photo restoration by Blackstar Studio, Chelmsford
Cover concept by Paul Dunning
Cover design by Carliam
Typeset by Carliam, 01707 659028
Printed on acid free paper by Good News Digital Books – Stevenage

The publishers are grateful to:
Holly Noonan for editing and proofreading

Published By:
Merlin Massara Publishing
(An imprint of Gilbert Massara Publishing)
www.gmpub.co.uk

Dedication

To Mum and Dad – Thank you for everything…

Contents

Acknowledgements

This is a story of a hero, as far as possible in his own words. The main part of our father's story is taken from his diary, letters, newspaper reports and contemporary pictures to which we have added explanatory commentary where necessary.

The main source of information in this book came from our mother, Mrs Veronica Young, who over the years collected, collated and kept all the information of my father's exploits in the hope that one day his story would be told. Thanks Mum.

We give special thanks to the nursing staff of The Erskine Ex-Servicemen and Woman's Hospital, who cared so well for my father during the last days of his life.

We would also like to thank Mr D.McKinnon (RAF) for his help in sourcing the publisher of this book. Also without Gilbert Massara and his colleagues, this story would not be told. Thank you all.

Alan Young

The publishers are grateful to:

Mrs D E Parker Housby, Head of Media & Communication and Mr A Nettleton, Deputy Head of Media & Communication for the Air Cadet Organisation, RAF Cranwell. Also to Flight Lieutenant V E Nicholls RAFVR(T), OC 49f (Greenock) Sqn, Air Training Corps – for their support with ATC information, advice and help with permissions to use insignia and crests.

Steve Gledhill, Gledhill Marketing Services – for his additional background, archive research and newspaper contact.

Air Britain (Historical) Ltd and Anthony Jones PR Director – for permission to reproduce the entry from their 1989 publication: 'The Hampden File' by Harry Moyle (ISBN 0851301282).

The Greenock Telegraph (Clyde & Forth Press Ltd) – for their kind permission to reproduce newspaper extracts.

G.M.

Foreword

This is a story of spirit, love and determination when our mother and father met in 1939, and were re-united in 1945.

The main part of this story has been taken from our father's diary notes, while being a POW from 1940 until 1945. As you will read, after meeting our mother in May 1939 he was shot down over France in December of that year. He would then spend the rest of the war trying to escape from various POW camps which would eventually lead to him being awarded the Military Cross for bravery.

In 1940 mother joined the Land Girls. These girls were given a uniform and worked hard on various duties and were paid 32 shillings a week (£1.60) for all their efforts. She then joined the Army Driving Corps and was there until liberation day on May 7th 1945.

Our father's Odyssey – his 'Long March Home'– is amazing; but in the end he made it and came back home in May 1945. During November 1945 David and Veronica were married in Stamford and then, after a lot of sole searching David decided to leave the RAF and go back to his home town in Greenock, Scotland. He rejoined the Company that he worked for before the war and aspired to be a manager with the firm. In 1947 a son was born and in 1951 a daughter.

We hope you enjoy the journey on The Long March Home.

Alan Young and Pat Young McEwan
December 2011.

Chapter 1

My Odyssey

By David Young (M.C.)

THE BEGINNING OF MY JOURNEY
RAF Scampton – 6th December 1940

A cold wintry morning, with snow forecast. However, the good news was that at our early morning briefing we were told to prepare for a bombing raid in France. A relatively short trip compared with the German raids we had been involved in over the past months.

The morning test flight had been completed, and at mid-day we reported for the final briefing on bomb loads, weather reports, intelligence, etc. A map was on display of an area, south of Paris, and all we needed now was the target.

The Wing Commander took his place beside the map, and then the good news turned to bad. Our mission was to seek out Luftwaffe training airfields, come down, bomb and strafe the airfields, and shoot down as many enemy aircraft as possible.

So we took off on what we knew was almost an impossible task, and as it turned out, a mission from which we would not return.

The temperature was below freezing, and snow was falling as we headed south towards the French coast. The coastal guns caused no damage to our Hampden bomber as we crossed into France. As we broke through the cloud base, at 2000 feet, we found our target lit up and training aircraft on the circuit. We entered the circuit to shoot down as many planes as possible, then unloaded our bombs on the airfields and hangers.

The defending flak guns opened up and many shells struck us without wounding any of the crew, so we climbed up quickly in the direction of England. But then both engines started losing power, and

Aircrew trainees, 1939

Ardmore House Hotel, 1939. Taken over by government to accommodate RAF recruits

David Young, 1940, aged 21,
prior to leaving Scampton on
operations.

Veronica Deegan, 1941,
aged 18.

Stalag 1, 1941, Germany, Barth.

it seemed probable that the fuel tanks had been hit, which could result in us crashing into the freezing cold English Channel. From this our chances of survival would be almost nil.

Our pilot, John Shaw, decided to turn south and head towards the Spanish border, so that when we crashed, or baled out, we would have a better chance of evading capture, and perhaps reaching Gibraltar, and eventually England.

However, our prospects of a visit to the south of France began to fade as our two damaged engines continued to lose power, and as we were already too close to the ground to safely escape by parachute, our pilot ordered us to take up our crash positions... there would be no Christmas for us this year.

As we approached ground through the clouds, some fifty miles south of Paris, we were heading directly towards a large forest. Our Hampden crashed into the trees, both wings were ripped off, but the fuselage carried on until it bounced out of the wood, and came to rest in deep snow.

I scrambled out of the wreckage and checked on the crew. They were unconscious and injured so I needed help to get them out, and receive medical attention. I could see a light across the fields and it turned out to be a French farmhouse. They managed to get the crew out and brought them to the farm.

The Germans dealt very harshly with anyone harbouring prisoners. In fact, they would almost certainly have been shot, or imprisoned, so I had to ask that the Germans be informed.

Shortly afterwards a group of German soldiers arrived and took us away to a local hospital, where the crew were taken to a surgical unit, and I was in a general ward. My mind was racing around in circles, and I thought about my girlfriend, Vee, who I had promised to meet in The Willow café on the night of the 7th. And here I was in a French hospital, with a German guard at the foot of my bed, and I could speak neither French nor German. My mind could take no more and I think I passed out.

Someone was shaking me, and not very gently, so I tried to pull myself together. I opened my eyes and confronting me was this German officer who was definitely not at all friendly, and he asked,

'Your bomber has crashed some miles from here, and after inspection there is a delayed action bomb under the wing… I want to know when it is primed to explode?'

I duly gave him my name, rank, number… and stopped. All hell then broke loose. 'If this bomb goes off and any of the soldiers guarding the wreck are killed, then you and your crew will also die.' 'Not a very good beginning,' I thought, but I really had no knowledge of the bomb device or its timing. It should have been dropped over the airfield we attacked, but we had been badly hit by flak and possibly there had been a malfunction of the mechanism.

The Gestapo officer stormed out of the ward, and I thought, 'My God, what is next in store for me?'

I must have slept for some time, I don't know how long, but someone was gently shaking my shoulders, and whispering in French. I thought I was dreaming. I opened my eyes, and bending over me was an elderly lady dressed in white. My first thought was, 'I am dead and she is an angel.' Then I thought, 'Why is she speaking in French?' So as I came to life she whispered to me, pointed to the window behind me, then pointed to her watch at a certain hour. She clasped my hand and left.

The next morning a French orderly told me she was a Countess working for the Résistance and was arranging for my escape. My crew were still in the surgical ward, and unable to get out of their beds. A German officer then came to tell me that he was taking me under guard to Germany immediately, so but for my bad French I may have escaped.

Worst was still to come. Having been driven to Paris, in the station I asked to go to the toilet, and no sooner had I entered I was approached by a Frenchman who pointed to another exit and obviously wanted me to make a run for it with him. Unfortunately the German officer had put a guard at each exit, and despite a chase through the crowded station, my brave French friend got away.

The officer was not at all happy about the incident, but I pointed out that it was my duty to escape, and this he accepted. After a long train journey up the Rhine valley we changed trains at Luxemburg, where the German officer took me to a beer garden to await the arrival of the train to take us to Frankfurt-on-Maine. I was offered a German beer, and wondered... 'Where to now?'

The next day we arrived in Frankfurt, and I was escorted to an International complex, prior to being taken to the prison camp. The camp was called Dulag Luft. The interrogation officer was efficient, offering me a cigarette, and questioning me about my squadron, number of aircraft, and so on. I quoted my name, rank, and number to every question and was taken to a very cold cell for the night, and the next day it was the same procedure.

After three days in the cell I was eventually taken off to the main camp, and had my first glimpse of what a prison camp really was: barbed wire, German guards and dogs everywhere.

Stalag Luft III – Sagan – 1943

A camp built in Silesia between Berlin and Breslau, and it was as grim as we imagined it to be. We arrived in January, and everything was covered in thick snow.

Escape in these conditions was impossible. To the east was Poland, German troops were massing in the west, north was the port of Stettin on the Baltic, and south crossing the Austrian border was Switzerland. So when the winter snows melted, these were the options to be considered.

Prisoners of War included such great war heroes as Douglas Bader, Stanford Tuck, Roger Bushell, Major Dodge, and many more who had already risked their lives for their country, yet their ultimate objective was to get back to their squadrons and carry on where they left off.

It is worthwhile considering that there were about ten thousand RAF Prisoners of War, and many spent more time in prison camps than on squadron duty. It is also worth noting that there were three types of guards: The Luftwaffe or German Air Force guards, who on the whole were fair and reasonable. Then there were the Gestapo guards, the Waffins who were elite fighting troops. And finally there was the SS Siuierhitdienst who were hooligans and criminals. They looked after the extermination camps and any other dirty jobs required.

On 25th March 1944 the well planned break out from Sagan took place when seventy six POWs escaped through a tunnel, and only three made it home. Thirteen were recaptured, and of these five were sent to a concentration camp. Fifteen were returned to Barth camp, and fifty were murdered by the Gestapo. A memorial to this terrible act is preserved by the Poles, near Sagan.

Before the escape took place I had been returned to Barth with a group of prisoners, and heard the full story there.

At Sagan I had a very memorable experience, one which is firmly etched in my mind, and which had a most remarkable effect on several prisoners who had in recent months been suffering from acute periods of deep depression and melancholia. From these depths it was virtually impossible to lift their spirits. They never spoke, neither did they mix with friends, really down in the pit of despair. It was worrying to see, and watch their effect on the rest of us.

And so back to my story… One cold winter's morning I went outside to the wash room, which was really just a toilet with basins, which never had toilet paper, soap, or towels. Simply a place to splash one's face, complete your ablutions, and get out as quickly as possible. So there I was making the best of a bad job when I noticed in the basin a few drops of blood. I knew it wasn't mine as I had not attempted to shave, but a few more spots appeared in the basin. Looking up at the roof I saw the stains and got out to find a guard.

I brought him in and showed him the blood, and asked him to report the matter quickly and get medical assistance. There was a British army doctor prisoner in the camp who very quickly arrived on the scene and got up on the roof to find a RAF navigator, who in one of his depressed states had found some broken glass and decided to end his life by cutting his throat. The doctor stopped the bleeding and the navigator was taken away for treatment by a German medic.

The interesting sequel to this story was that the army doctor arranged for all POWs to gather in the compound, and also the navigator who was bandaged around the throat, but more or less in one piece. And so the doctor asked us to pay attention, and then produced a knife. He then spoke: 'That man sitting there wanted to die, but he made a complete cock up of the attempt.' Holding aloft the knife for all to see he went on, 'I shall now demonstrate to all of you the mistake he made, just in case any of you are weak enough in mind and spirit to try and end your life. The mistake most suicidal people make is to tilt their head backwards and then cut their throat. Totally wrong, because you fail to cut the artery. The correct way is to put your head on your chest, and then cut. You will sever the artery and death will follow quickly if you are certain that is your desire.'

I looked around me and saw the people I thought had that exit from life in mind, and in my travels, and to my knowledge, there were never any recorded suicides, or attempted suicides.

The doctor knew his shock tactics would do the trick and improve morale, which it certainly did.

During one of my abortive attempts to escape I was captured and locked up in a labour camp, where there were POWs from Holland, France, and Poland. They were working in factories, building sites, farms, in fact anywhere there was a shortage of manual workers. As I was not allowed by the Geneva Convention to work, arrangements were made to have me returned to the camp from which I had escaped. The accommodation was filthy, lice infected, and primitive. In my brief stay I saw a British soldier obviously suffering extreme pain, and as I went over to him I could smell the unmistakable odour of gangrene. I don't know too much about medicine, but I did know the affected leg must be amputated to save his life.

I said so to the guard and asked to see an officer to tell him the situation. He said that all the medical matters were dealt with by a French doctor, whom I demanded to see. This surgeon appeared and I explained the seriousness of this soldier's condition and to my amazement he asked me how much I could give him before he operated. I went mad with him even referring to his oath to save lives, but to no avail... he was adamant. In the end I gave him my Irvine flying jacket and then he agreed. The soldier was carried to the makeshift hospital and returned sometime later with his leg amputated. During that night I never left his side and when he awoke I will never forget his words. In a whisper he said, 'David, if I come through this do you think I could, after the war, join the RAF?' 'Well of course,' I assured him. These were the last words he spoke as his life was ebbing away and I could do nothing. An army corporal came up to the bed, stuck a cigarette paper on his upper lip and said, 'When the paper stops moving his breathing will have stopped, and he has gone.'

The movement of the paper stopped, and I swore if I came through the war I would expose this French surgeon for operating only for money, jewellery, or any other goods.

And I am pleased to complete this episode by recounting that when I was interrogated by MI5 on my return, this story of my young soldier friend was recounted, and the so-called surgeon reported. As a matter of fact, MI5 had already been informed, from other sources, and no doubt this charlatan received his just rewards.

Barth

A new camp built on the Baltic coast to accommodate the increasing number of aircrew being shot down and taken prisoner. The only escape routes were either to get to one of the German ports to the east, or somehow get across the twenty miles of the Baltic to Sweden. It was virtually impossible to escape at this time of year and most attempts usually ended in recapture. It was regarded by the Germans as part of camp routine, which was punishable by a spell of solitary confinement.

My pilot, who had recovered from his injuries, tried to crawl across the snow and cut his way through the wire. All was going well until a sentry spotted him with his search light and called out to John to halt, which he did, raising his hands in surrender. The guards then overreacted and shot him dead. The Germans realised the gravity of the incident and decreed that John's body should be buried with full military honours. John was a good pilot, and a personal friend, and died a hero's death doing his duty for his country.

One day I remember very well, I was sitting alone in a small room reading, making notes, and listening to Hitler giving one of his frequent speeches (which were broadcasted all day, every day). A German Captain came in and sat beside me. He spoke good English and told me he had been a professor at Heidelberg University when he was drafted into the administration section of the army. Then he told me how the war had disrupted his life, and so on.

On many occasions we talked and covered music, culture, how the war had changed so many things in the world; and then the subject came up about the Jewish Question. He asked me if I had ever heard

Stalag 1, 1941, Germany, Barth.

Stalag 3, 1942, Poland, Sagan.
Camp band leader, Bill Baird
enjoying potato peel wine.

Stalag 3, 1942, Poland, Sagan.
David sampling the potato peel wine.

Stalag 3, 1942, Poland, Sagan.

Stalag 3, 1942, Poland, Sagan. Bill Baird and his merry band

Stalag 3, 1942, Poland, Sagan.

Stalag 3, 1942, Poland, Sagan. The funeral of David's friend and pilot J.C.Shaw who was shot attempting escape.

Steenberg, 1945. Davids last prison.

of 'Kristallnacht.' I replied no. Then he went on to tell me the whole sordid story, which I will relate just as it was told to me:

Kristallnacht – The Night of the Broken Glass
10th November 1938

In Paris a German diplomat had been shot by a Polish Jew, who had been expelled from Germany, and Herr Hitler wanted reprisals... Kristallnacht was ordered. Every window in every shop belonging to Jews throughout Germany was broken. Jews on the street were beaten with clubs and chains, robbed of all their possessions, and then imprisoned. All books and rare manuscripts written by the Jews were destroyed. Their homes and synagogues burned, and the women were brutally raped and humiliated.

The fanatical members of the SS and Gestapo wanted Jewish blood, and afterwards the Jews were transferred to concentration camps, where their tortures continued.

It was at Barth that I first came to take stock of my position. I accepted that the war was certainly not going to be over quickly, and that I must use the time at my disposal to increase my knowledge of many subjects. The sense of feeling sorry for myself was over, and no one but I could do anything about it. I was in the company of young men from all walks of life, from many countries, and I was sadly lacking in many areas of intelligence. Now was my chance to improve myself.

Every opportunity I had I was in quest of knowledge and my questions were freely answered on every subject under the sun. In the fullness of time I quenched my thirst, but as I grew up mentally a non-emotional barrier was being built inside me which was necessary for my survival. I was becoming a different person, one I had created, but one I did not like very much. I had tried to wipe out mentally the memories of the world I had left behind, there could be no room for sentimental thoughts in my new world, and so attempts to erase the past and occupy my mind became an obsession.

Stalag Luft VI – Heydekrug – East Prussia – 1944

An isolated and remote area a few miles from Lithuania and the Baltic port of Memel. The winters were long and the icy winds from Siberia continuously swept across the camp. It was colder than one could imagine and lack of food and warm clothing were becoming very serious problems. The potato ration was being reduced daily and vegetables were unknown.

The Red Army were getting closer and their guns were clearly heard night and day. The order had been received from the German high command to evacuate the camp immediately. The following morning we were marched to the nearest railway station and were locked up in cattle trucks, fifty men to a truck, for a journey to Memel where we were to board a prison ship called Insterberg. On the dockside, looking at this rusty old coal boat, I could not help thinking that this was going to be the worst day of my life. I could not have been more wrong. The nightmare days to follow were without doubt to be the most horrendous I was ever to experience in my life. In retrospect it is perhaps not wise to know one's future.

We climbed the ladder to the deck, and then down a rope ladder to the hold. It was dark and hot and we were like sardines. There were so many of us that we were three deep in the bowels of this filthy, stinking ship. Sleep was out of the question, no toilets, no beds, no food, and we had to urinate in a bucket, to be passed aloft from head to head. If something banged against the hull you said a prayer as it could be a mine. After three days and nights Insterberg docked at the navel base of Swinemunde, and we marched along the dockside to our now familiar cattle trucks.

At some point the guard from our next camp took charge, and told us we were all to be put in chains. We were shackled in twos, hand and foot, and the train pulled out of Swinemunde. We were by now hungry, filthy, tired, worn, and hoped it would not be too long before we reached our next camp, and perhaps be able to lie down. It was not to be. The train came to a halt at Kiefcheidr, a small farming area in Poland. The journey had been long, standing in cattle trucks for twenty four hours, and we were looking forward to having our shackles removed and the chance to wash and rest.

We stood at the siding under the blazing sun for a long time, then appeared young navy personnel with fixed bayonets, SS guards with dogs, and Gestapo officers. An SS officer started shouting, 'Macht

Schnell!' (quick march), and then the trouble really started. 'You are going to run all the way to the camp,' the officer was screaming. We were hardly capable of walking at this stage, but the young navy boys then started prodding us with their bayonets, and smashing their rifle butts on our backs and legs. Each time they would jab us they would call out the name of a German town that had been bombed.

Worse was to come as the dogs were then unleashed and started biting at us. Many prisoners went down because of their shackles and were badly mauled by the dogs while on the ground. The march westward was moving slowly, and the prisoners were not physically capable of walking any faster. We were being pushed along in the snow like zombies with barely enough food to keep us alive. One night I was lying in a field with my comrades and a German guard came up and spoke to me, 'You are not very far from a town called Ludviglost and there are no other roads, so the column will have to go through. The town has suffered very heavy air attacks by the Americans and British and a great number of the town's people have been killed. There will be many attacks on you, and perhaps some of you will die, and we will not be able to do anything about it.' With these ominous words he went off on his rounds.

By this time it had become clear that the whole thing was planned to incite us to attempt to escape. All along the woods on each side the German soldiers were ready to open up on us. They wanted us to panic, and then cut us down, and photographers were ready to film the whole incident. I don't think they imagined we could hold together like we did. The guards were hurling insults, spitting, ripping our possessions from us, and degrading us in every way, but we kept on running. We had survived the dreaded 'Hydekrug Run,' organised to kill us. For three days we had eaten virtually nothing, had no sleep, been huddled up choking in a stinking ship, been beaten, humiliated, and forced to run in chains… but we showed them how young airmen got it right by facing them and winning the fight.

So bruised, battered, and bleeding we eventually reached the camp after an hour's run. The camp was called Gross Tychow and it was obvious we had not been expected to reach there. No huts, no beds, no medication, and no food. We lay in a field for two days until tents arrived, and some straw. We were alive, but only just. There were a thousand men at the start of this march, I wondered how many there were now. We covered six hundred and twenty miles in ten weeks with little food, mostly cold potatoes and some raw turnips from the fields. When we rested by night on the icy ground many died of starvation and disease. Dead horses were a source of food, and even grass.

Escape from the Death March

Lying there I reached probably the most important decision of my life: It wasn't too difficult, either to carry on and become progressively weaker with the additional risk of being stoned to death, hanged, or suffer some similar fate. Or the alternative, which would be to break away from the column while I still had some strength and retrace my steps by travelling eastwards, in the hope that I would eventually make contact with the advancing Russian army. The decision had to be the latter. Escaping from the column at night presented no problems, as the guards were tired and many had been wounded on the eastern front, and many had lost their appetite for war... The die had been cast.

Each day I would ask at Farmhouses for food and water, finding the people pitiable but very friendly. After a day or two I felt it safe enough to say that I was RAF and the effect was invariably gratifying. They gave me what food they could, usually a few potatoes, and sometimes a little bread, but that was not very much as they had little themselves. I had never seen such poor people, many dressed in shawls or dresses that they had made themselves, and there were practically no men left in the villages. Although I had made good progress I knew I was getting weaker and tiring myself physically and mentally. I was not thinking positively or sensibly. I had to re-adjust my whole attitude without advice or knowledge, but the instinct of survival is strong and inherent in every human and animal.

After a few days I let my guard down and became overconfident. I approached a house and the door was opened by a German soldier who asked many questions I was not able to answer, and I did not fully understand. I had to say escaping British prisoner and I showed him my identity discs. I had braced myself to bluff it out, and now it was all over without a show or fight. For a moment or two I thought I was about to die as he had produced a gun, but he gave instructions to another soldier who left the house, and within a short time I was in a cell in a nearby town. German army officers then appeared and took me off to a prison camp called 'Thorne.

This camp was used to send out working parties and all the POWs were British army. After interrogation I gave my name, rank, and number and was again put in a cell. I was obviously an embarrassment as I wasn't allowed to work because I was RAF, however it was decided to send me with an army Sergeant, a Corporal, and eighteen men to a working camp called Sternberg.

Sternberg – March 1945

This was a small country town in northern Germany. We arrived at the station and there to meet us was a small group of civilians, including the local Mayor. The guards had a few words with them and the German officer told me that from now on we would be working in the fields, forests, and farms, wherever manual work was required. We would be taking the place of the men folk who had been recruited by the army. With these words he and our guards boarded the train, and left. The Mayor told me to follow him to where we would be billeted, and off he went through the narrow streets. Many people were watching us without any expression in their faces. We stopped shortly and the Mayor said, 'This is where you will stay.'

I could hardly believe my eyes, no barbed wire, no guards, no dogs, and no bars on the windows. The building was a shooting lodge part of which was used by the town officials, and we were in another section. Bunk beds, blankets, running water, and cooking facilities, it was unbelievable… perhaps my luck had changed. The Mayor came in and told me to report to him in the morning to outline our duties. I took the Sergeant with me and he sorted out a roster of the jobs, and off the group went to their various locations.

Now Sternberg had no particular military significance, except that it straddled the direct and only route of the advancing Red Army to meet up with the allied forces. Now in addition to our working party there were women and girls from Polish, French, and Jewish forced labour camps working nearby, and this caused our first real problem. One day one of our men working in the woods came across a young Polish girl with a German soldier, and the inevitable occurred. Her guard came across them and the situation became very nasty. He reported this to the Mayor who pointed out how serious this matter was, and I told the men what he had told me. After a week or two I was told to take the men to the town square where he would be waiting. The square was dominated by a statue of Kaiser William, and on one side of the statue there was hanging a German soldier, and on the other a Jewish girl. Underneath was a notice reading, *'Fraternising with the Enemy is Punishable by Death'*.

After that incident there was a cooling off period, and then matters took a new turn. The American and RAF were flying overhead day and night en route to Berlin. And the Russian Air Force were starting to bomb the coastal road on which we were. The Mayor then made a wise decision. 'We have decided,' he said, 'to ask all the townspeople to sleep in the fields at night, and you and your men must join them for safety.' So the war had taken a new turn, from being resented and rejected by the locals we were now going to lie down beside them, and share their fears. The 'no fraternising' policy was now ignored, and I didn't dare ask any of the men who they had lain down beside, but there were no complaints by anyone.

One morning the Mayor, looking very worried, came to see me. 'Will you come with me into the town centre?' he said. Down we went and I saw it, a large unexploded Russian bomb. 'I would consider it a great favour if you could arrange for this bomb to be taken out of the town. If it explodes we shall all be killed or injured, including yourselves, and if you can dispose of it we shall be forever in your debt.' So I had to break the news and the request to the squad, that time was running out fast, and that it may have a delayed action mechanism for all I knew.

So I put the dilemma to the men, and their response was immediate: get rid of it. A hay cart was found and the bomb was gingerly lifted onto a bed of hay. It was pulled to a clearing out of town using ropes, where after a short time it went off. Whether it was the movement of transporting it, or a timing device, we will never know. Even now I can remember the incident as though it was yesterday, every bump on that rough road I thought was the end, and I don't think I have ever been so scared in my life.

As I have said, air attacks went on night after night and the Russian guns were getting nearer. The road through the town was packed with people fleeing from the Russians, and hundreds of retreating German soldiers were heading west. So the time had come to make decisions, whether to stay and risk being killed in the raids by Russian fighter bombers, or head west to try and make contact with the allied forces, or go eastwards to meet up with the Russians. All three options carried equal risks, and so one night we held a long discussion and the decision was reached. My army comrades elected to go west, and I elected to try to contact the Russians.

There was no question of escaping, we just had to walk away on our separate roads. We had ample food and water, and so I bid farewell to my friends, and as dawn broke we shook hands and set off. I got up into the hills above Sternberg and into the forest where I could clearly see the main road, and just kept walking. Some time later I was deep into the wood at night and heard the sound of gunfire for sometime, then silence. In the morning I came across the bodies of German SS officers who had apparently committed suicide, the reason being possibly that the Russian army never took prisoners all throughout the war.

Well, I thought I had gone far enough and within a few hours I heard the sound of tanks, and decided this was as good a time as any to give myself up. So I walked across a field towards the road with my hands up and my heart pounding. One tank halted and a soldier came down to approach me. He had medals on both sides of his uniform and was wearing a black fur hat. He shouted at me and not knowing any Russian except the word for 'comrade,' I used that and said, 'RAF,' keeping one hand up and producing my RAF identity disk. He motioned me to keep both my hands up and called out to someone in the column to speak to me in English.

This officer came up and asked questions about where I had come from, and whether Sternberg was defended, and so on. The tension eased and he shook my hand warmly, gave me a hug, laughed, and produced a flask of Vodka. We had a toast to the collapse of Germany and he took me inside his tank. And so the Russian advancing continued, and for the first time in four years I was free, and barring accidents, I was on my way home.

Life with the Russians

To say the least it was a most remarkable experience, and I was to have many surprises as time went by. When the column stopped I was taken for a walk among the troops in the nearby fields and gazed fascinated at the number of female soldiers who were lying down to sleep among the other male soldiers. The Russian officer explained they are our comrades, there is no sex in battle, and there is never any trouble with the men. They all seemed to be in good spirits, laughing and joking among themselves. My friend had found me a Russian uniform of sorts, and he said that in the morning the tanks would enter the next town and would ask if they wanted to fight or surrender.

By mid-day the tanks, soldiers, and Cossacks were in position and a shell was fired in the air above the town. Shortly afterwards the local Mayor appeared waving a white flag. One tank took him down to the town centre where it took up position, and the townspeople were told that they were now under Russian control. The tank I was in with around six others drove into the town and this is when the situation became unbelievable to me. I was motioned to follow my officer and we approached a house, the door was kicked in and the people were told to put all their valuables on the table, and then stand against the wall. Next the officers sorted out all the watches, jewellery, or whatever they wanted, and asked me to help myself to which I declined.

And then they turned to the women and girls and decided who they wanted, and again I had to refuse. Thereupon the whole room turned into a sex orgy with women screaming and crying. Then the officers carted off the girls of their choice, their loot, some bottles of spirits, and we got back into the tanks and drove back to the camp. I was shocked at this behaviour and had to remonstrate with the officer. 'Don't you worry,' he remarked, 'the soldiers are now on their way into town, and will enjoy themselves, and tomorrow our advance continues'… I don't think he understood what I meant.

As we reached every town the format was the same and the news had obviously gone on ahead because every village and every town surrendered rather than being totally destroyed. One day we were making our way through a town with very narrow streets and there was not very much room for the tanks to negotiate the corners. Anyway one of the tanks got jammed and blocked the road completely. A high ranking female, wearing the uniform of a commissar (which meant she was superior to all Russian army officers), appeared on the scene. She pulled out her revolver and promptly shot dead the driver responsible. Another driver was ordered to take over and we carried on, leaving the dead driver on the pavement. Like I say, it was all unreal to me but accepted by everyone else… I was free, but in a position I could not get out of.

I remembered reading an account of Hannibal on his journeys, where he looted, raped, and pillaged, in just the same way as the Russians. My comrade told me one night that we were not very far away from the allied forces, and when I was handed over they would receive a reward. I can't remember the sum but later I got confirmation that this was true and I believe it took the form of an IOU payable after the war by the British government. One day the two armies met up and there was quite a celebration, shaking hands and toasting the victory.

I was taken away in a staff car to a town called Lubeck, on the coast, and although there were pockets of resistance the town of Lubeck was in their hands. I was taken away by an officer of the airborne division to a block of luxury apartments where he shot the lock off the door, and said to me, 'Have a good bath, a good sleep, and I shall call for you in the morning.' So I could sleep in a proper bed for the first time in years, it then struck me that I was really free, and could relax. In the morning I went with the officer to have something to eat, and he told me I would have to travel to Luneburg, a good bit south where command headquarters had been set up. There was a big airfield in Luneburg but the Germans had blocked the runways with tanks, cars, etc., so I couldn't get out by air. The officer picked up a private car, filled it up with petrol, gave me a map and revolver, and I set off south.

The final stage of my Odyssey

I was driving again after all these years… I had an army uniform, ample food, and although the car was a left hand drive and the roads were in a bad state, with shell holes, and abandoned cars and trucks all over the place, I had plenty of time and took it easy. I met up with an American patrol one day, and they asked me to follow them as they were going to a concentration camp, which had just been liberated, and they wanted me to see, as a witness, what had been going on there. We arrived at the camp and went on a tour of inspection.

The memory of what I saw there will remain in my thoughts forever: hundreds of Jews lying dead, a number still alive, but with dying hands outstretched to clasp ours. They were too far gone to eat, or even have a cigarette, and the smell of death from decaying corpses was overpowering. The men still alive were living skeletons, riddled with tuberculosis, and weighing only a few stones. But they were happy to see us with their vacant eyes. I went to the washing area and the bodies were stacked high row upon row. A US army photographer was making a film of the carnage, with the spikes on the tripods piercing the bodies. I wasn't too happy about this, but he said it was important to film the scene, and there wasn't an inch of space left to set up the cameras.

I continued on my journey, and after this episode just hoping that the people responsible would eventually be brought to trial and shot, every guilty one. Whether that has happened I don't know, but I have a strong suspicion that many of them were never brought to justice.

So I continued on my way, crossing the Elber on pontoons as the retreating Germans had blown up the bridges, and I eventually found my way to Luseburg. Many liberated POWs had already arrived, and there were many emotional reunions. It was there that I learned with sorrow that a large number of my friends had been killed on the Dead March, after I escaped, unfortunately by RAF fighter bombers who had apparently mistaken the column of POWs for retreating Germans. It was a cruel twist of fate that after many years in captivity so many young airmen were destined to die by RAF fire… It must have some meaning but it escapes me… perhaps part of the Grand Design?

After a time we were issued with uniforms, we knew we were going home, but it was difficult to comprehend. I was told by a friend that I should have continued driving south into France where I could have sold my car at a large price because of the shortages. I could have lived in France for a while, and then reported to the occupational forces who would fly me to England... But at that time nothing mattered to me more than getting back home.

The next surprise came when we were told that there wasn't an airfield in the area suitable for getting any number of RAF planes in. We were going to be driven up to Lubeck, where the landing strips had been cleared of debris, and RAF Lancaster bombers would land to airlift us home.

So after that long journey by car from Lubeck, here I was on my way back there again. Back in Lubeck we again went into private flats to sleep and get ready for our flight. The next day I saw the Lancasters coming into land, and I could hardy believe how big they were, and the engines sounded so powerful. I sat on the grass with my comrades and looked at the planes fuelling up and started to wonder about many things.

Somewhere, sometime I had changed, I had lost my youth, and I had become cold inside. Situations had left their mark on me, could I quickly adjust to a different environment, or could I adjust at all?

Questions without answers... I had grown up in many ways, learned a lot, perhaps more than I ever learned at school. But in the process I had lost something and didn't know whether I could ever recover it. So I boarded the Lancaster no wiser, only time would tell.

The engines revved up to take off (what power!), and we were airborne and heading home.

I wondered if Vee was still unmarried, or married with children... had her feelings changed... could we start again?

I wondered and worried all through the flight, and then the east coast of England was in sight, we reduced height, and came into land.

The wheels touched down, and I was home, my Odyssey was over... I had completed a full circle.

A new life awaited me out there...

David Young

Chapter 2

Meeting David

By Veronica Young (nee Deegan)

Stamford – Early evening – June 1940

It was purely fate. I had written a letter to my brother, who was in India, and I wanted to get away as soon as I could.

As I was walking to the Post Office I met one of my friends, Diana. She joined me and we were so busy talking we almost bumped into two young RAF men, and to my astonishment Diana knew one of them.

She was laughing and talking to the man she knew, whose name was Jack. His friend David and I were left just gazing at each other. Diana introduced me to Jack and David introduced himself. Diana and Jack were going for a drink, David said he was hungry and he invited me for a meal.

I took him to an excellent place called the Willow Cafe. It was one of these 'Ye Olde' cafes with furnishing to match and excellent food. We had arrived at six o'clock and before we knew it, the time was ten o'clock. We were talking the whole time and we were comfortable in each other's company, there was no shyness.

David told me of his life in Scotland and about his training in Cranwell. We were also speaking about seeing each other again. But it was not going to be easy as David was based at an airfield in a village called Cottesmore, which was about twenty miles from where I lived, and it was impossible to get transport to there. As it turned out he hitchhiked to see me mostly.

Apart from the air raids and David flying (weather permitting), we could not have been happier

Wedding Photo 1945, October 1st, Stamford.

David and family 1999, at a local hotel in Greenock

December 7th 1940

We had made arrangements to meet in the Willow Cafe at 7pm and I had arrived on time. A little later one of David's friends, that I knew from his squadron, came over to my table. He sat down and took my hand and said, 'Vee I have some bad news, David is missing presumed killed. I was on the same operation and we saw David's plane getting hit by flak, and we could see they were in a bad state. We followed them, and they didn't have enough height to use their parachutes. In another few minutes they had crashed into a forest and we didn't see any movement around the crash spot.'

I cannot remember walking home that night, and I could just not believe David was dead. There was no way I could get any information on the crash, but I did know that 'presumed killed' was not final. I just had to hope for the best.

A few weeks later I received a letter from David's mother. In it she told me that on New Year's Eve she was listening to a broadcast from Germany by 'Haw Haw,' and he said, 'I have a message for Mr and Mrs Young,' and gave their address. He continued, 'Warrant Officer Young is a Prisoner of War in Germany.'

What a great relief for his family, and for me!!!

Shortly after this good news I received a small card from David saying he thought the war would last a very long time. He said he wanted me to forget about him, live my life, and enjoy myself.

I was very hurt about this for some time, then I realised what it must have cost him to have sent the card. He must have been very unhappy.

Time went by and in the following year (1942) I joined the A.T.S. and trained as a driver. I was then posted to Colchester and became a driver in the Royal Army Service Corps, I really enjoyed that experience.

May 1944

I was home on leave and a letter came for me, and it turned out it was from David.

Apparently he had spent some time in hospital when he arrived back in Britain, and he would be coming to see me the following Wednesday.

I was feeling rather nervous that day, and then eventually the doorbell rang. I opened the door and we just fell into each others arms and cried.

In June that year we got engaged and set our wedding date for October. I got demobilised and David managed to get a posting to another airfield (Wittering), near my home. We were both so happy to be together again.

On August 25th David was awarded with the 'Military Cross' for his bravery, and on October 1st we were married, and going on honeymoon.

Veronica Young

Chapter 3

The Hampden File

ACKNOWLEDGMENTS

The information contained in "The Hampden File" has been gathered from four main sources; they are: –

1. Personal Accounts from ex – aircrew who flew on Hampdens and from the "erks" who serviced them.
2. Official Records.
3. Squadron Historians, Ex – Service Organisations, Researchers in the United Kingdom.
4. Overseas Researchers.

1. Personal accounts from ex – Hampden personnel:

The assistance received from those whose accounts are used in the book is gratefully acknowledged as is that from others who made contact about the Hampdens. Their interest provided a continual source of encouragement during the compilation of "The Hampden File". The names are grouped in their different aircrew categories and squadrons, and where practicable an index number is given of the relevant incident. It is hoped that they will forgive the omission of details of rank and decorations, etc.

Pilots :
44 Sqn:	Dave Penman 5H3; Tony Reid 2C9; Mike Lewis.
49 Sqn:	Des Dunphy 3D6; Bob Hamer (AT112); Lewis Hodges 3D31
50 Sqn:	'Abdul' Abbott (AE251); Jimmy Bennett; 'Weasel' Donaldson 2C15; George Potts 5B3; Chas Stenner; Gus Walker
61 Sqn:	Peter Tunstall 3D28; 'Spooky' Barrett 3D13
83 Sqn:	Stan Harpham 2K9; Freddie Newall 5B11; Leonard Snaith 2C; Neil Svendsen 5B2; Tony Stamer; Rod Learoyd VC.
106 Sqn:	Vic Cooper (AE123); Wally Huggins; Chas Lockyer; Roy Haggar; Roger Purnell, Robert Warring
144 Sqn:	Jimmy Bennett; Bob Galloway 2C2; Max Meyer; Bob Pearman 5A16; Colin Rawlins 2D11; Gordon Walters.
408 Sqn:	David Williams
415 Sqn:	Bill Adams 2J36; John Enns 2J37
420 Sqn:	Robert Kee 2D10
455 Sqn:	Grant Lindeman
A&AEE:	Tom Stanley
45 (Atlantic Transport) Group:	Maurice Ratcliffe

Air Observers, Air Gunner Officers, Navigators
44 Sqn:	Andrew Coveyduck 3D8; Gerrie Harris (P2077); Alan Nicoll
50 Sqn:	John Day 2G; Gil Haworth 2D, 5G6; W J Johnstone (P1202); George Leonard (L4046)
83 Sqn:	Julian Badcock 5A52
144 Sqn:	W D Barrett 2J7; Dave Withey; 'Timber' Woods 2K23; Vernon Smith
415 Sqn:	Jim Chapman; E.L.Rowe
455 Sqn:	Bob Anderson 2J7; Ray Lassiter (P1208)
32 OTU:	W N Switzer; P Moorhead Nav W/T.

Wireless Operator/Air Gunners and Air Gunners
44 Sqn:	Fred Ball; M Beale; Jim Taylor; Joe Dacey
49 Sqn:	Don Foster; David Young 3D26; John Fairbrother; 'Chan' Chandler 5B10
50 Sqn:	Geoff Ashmore; Fred Bailey 2D8; Doug Barrie 2K26; Nairn 'Robbie' Robertson 2G; Jim Mitchell; Bill Sykes
61 Sqn:	'Bernie' Bernard; Neil Prendergrast 2E2; Len Walker 3D2; John Brock 3D2
83 Sqn:	Eric Groves (L4057); Jack Lawrence 3D10; Hector Macdonald
106 Sqn:	Tom Berry (AE123); Jim Palmer (AE123); Allen Wiseman; George Luke 3D23
144 Sqn:	Bert Earl* 2J13; Bernard Sowerby * 2J12; * Both groundcrew who flew on Russia flight; Jim Rowland, groundcrew on Russia detachment
408 Sqn:	Don Foster
415 Sqn:	Doug Stallard
420 Sqn:	David Semple
455 Sqn:	George Baynes; Bill McPhee; John McKissack, groundcrew on Russia detachment
489 Sqn:	Guy Gaskill 3D24; Eric Cameron

2.Official Records

Public Record Office at Kew
The Record Books of Squadrons Stations, Groups and Commands, and many files on particular aspects of Hampden operations were researched.

Air Historical Branch, London.
Permission was obtained to study Hampden 'Crash' cards, 'Movement' cards and 'Contract' cards. The staff answered many written queries on Hampden fates.

RAF Museum, Hendon
The Museum photographic library proved to be a valuable source of photographs, and in the early stages of research Andrew Cormack offered information on crew fates. CWGC has to charge for Registers and queries on individual crew fates. The service received proved well worth the financial outlay.

The Imperial War Museum, London
The staff of the photographic library assisted in the selection of suitable photographs.

The Commonwealth War Graves Commission, Maidenhead
War Cemetery Registers and the Runnymede Memorial Register provided information on crew fates. CWGC has to charge for Registers and queries on individual crew fates The service received proved well worth the financial outlay.

Public Archives of Canada, Ontario and the Supply and Services Department, Ottawa proved to be valuable sources of good quality photographs. The courteous assistance given by the staff of all of the aforementioned Departments is acknowledged with gratitude.

Australian War Memorial, Canberra, answered several questions regarding aircraft and crew fates.

Bournemouth and Poole College of Art and Design
Sue Brown, a student at the Department of Technical Illustration, produced the cutaway drawing and several maps.

Air – Britain
Cliff Minney, the association's graphics adviser, produced the Hampden sideviews.

3.Squadron Historians and Ex – service Associations and Researchers in the United Kingdom

Ron Low and Frank Harper of 83 Squadron; John Farley and Des Richards of 106 Squadron; Gus Dodson and Frank Priestly of 61 Squadron; Kenneth Green of 61 Squadron and Hemswell; Bob Cotterill and Bill Boorer of 144 Squadron; Alan White and Bert Dowty of 44 Squadron and Ray Leach of 50 Squadron. Peter Green provided various photographs and assisted with the reproduction of others. 'Cee' Wadsworth provided photographs of 455 RAAF Squadron.

Ex – Service Organisations
Requests for information in newsletters of various ex – service organisations led to many Hampden contacts coming to light from The Aircrew Association, The Prisoner of War Association, the Royal Air Force Association, The Air Transport Auxiliary Association, The Handley Page Association, The Goldfish Club, The Air Sea Rescue/Marine Craft Club and the Lincolnshire Bomber Airfield Society. 'FlyPast' and 'Air – Britain Digest' were the two principal Aviation journals involved in seeking answers to particular problems.

Researchers in the United Kingdom
Brian Nicholls, who is engaged on the part – reconstruction of a Hampden at the Lincolnshire Aviation Heritage Centre at East Kirkby; Roy Nesbitt; Roger Hayward; Eric Thale; Mike Hodsman; Chaz Bowyer; John Foreman and Thomas E Willis who provided several interesting photographs, also corresponded.

27

P4404: A Crash Landing and its Consequences

On the night of 7/8 December 1940, P4404 (26) of 49 Squadron took off from Scampton; its mission was to seek out Luftwaffe training airfields to the south of Paris and attempt to emulate the success that the German "Intruder" aircraft of NJG/2 had achieved over England. The temperature was well below freezing and light snow was falling as they headed south from Scampton and with a weather forecast that included snow, ice and low cloud the crew could not have been over-optimistic about the chance of their mission achieving anything. Sergeant John Shaw, the pilot of P4404 must have thought that it was his lucky night when he actually found a German airfield, all nicely lit up and with aircraft in the circuit. No doubt with visions of a DFM floating before him, he entered the circuit with the object of shooting one of the Jerries down and then unloading his bombs on the hangars and buildings of tne airfield.

The inconsiderate Germans, however, had realised that there was a fox after their chickens. Their radar had probably tracked P4404 in from the coast, so when the aircraft headed in towards the airfield and came within range of the defending light flak guns, it received the full treatment. Streams of tracer poured up towards the Hampden and many shells struck the aircraft, fortunately without wounding any of the crew. When he was clear of the hail of shells, John took stock of the situation and deciding that the Hampden was too badly mauled to justify returning for more punishment he turned on to a northerly course in the general direction of England. Both engines began losing power; it seemed probable that the fuel tanks had been damaged, which could result in a ditching in the cold English Channel from which their chances of survival would be almost nil. John decided that a wiser plan would be to turn south and head towards the Spanish border, so that when they crash landed or baled out, they would have a better chance of evading capture and reaching Gibraltar and, eventually, good old England.

Just as the visions of a DFM had earlier come to nothing, the prospect of a visit to the south of France began to fade as the two stricken Pegasus engines continued to lose power. John Shaw, realising that they were already too close to the ground for the crew to escape safely by parachute, decided that a crash landing was the only possible course of action and ordered his crew to take up their crash positions. He eased P4404 down towards the ground which materialised in the form of a forest, some fifty miles south of Paris. The Hampden crashed down into the trees, the wings were ripped off but the fuselage continued gamely onwards through the trees until it bounced out of the wood and came to rest in a Field, which as David Young, one of the two wireless operators in the crew, remembered thankfully "was covered in deep snow". A French family from a nearby farm offered aid but, as some of the crew needed hospital treatment, the offer was declined, particularly as it was known that the Germans dealt harshly with anyone helping RAF aircrew to hide or escape. The crew asked that the Germans be informed of their presence and they were soon in the care of the enemy.

After they had recovered from their injuries the crew were moved to Stalag Luft, on the Baltic coast. David Young had no complaint about the manner in which they were treated at this time as although rations were meagre the Germans never resorted to physical punishment or torture. The attempts at escape from the camp usually ended in recapture and were regarded by their captors as part of the prison camp routine, for which the punishment was a ritual spell of solitary confinement.

Wing Commander "Wings" Day, the Senior British Officer at Stalag Luft, had established an escape committee and in due course John Shaw came up with a simple escape plan, which was to camouflage himself with a white sheet and then do an "Invisible Man" act to crawl across the snow to the wire fences surrounding the compound. He would then cut his way through the wire. The plan received the blessing of the Escape Committee and when it was put into operation all went quite well until a vigilant sentry, operating a searchlight on one of the look-out towers, spotted John cutting away at the wire. The sentry called out to one of the patrolling guards, who challenged John, who, realising that his bid for freedom had ended, raised his hands in surrender and turned to face the guard, who promptly shot him dead.

Whether the shooting had been accidental, maybe in a moment of panic, or as some feared, deliberate, was a matter of great concern to all the prisoners at Stalag Luft. The Germans too, seemed to be aware of the gravity of the incident, as they instituted a full enquiry and decreed that John Shaw's body should be buried with full military honours; David Young was present at the grave-side and sorrowfully remarked that, on this occasion, the rifles of the Luftwaffe Guard of Honour fired blank ammunition. He paid tribute to him thus, "John was a good pilot, and a very brave man. He died a hero's death, doing his duty for his country. I hope that his family have heard of the circumstances of his death."

David lost track of Pilot Officer B H Evans, the navigator of P4404, during his subsequent years of captivity. He was appalled to learn that he too had been shot by the Germans in an act of cold-blooded murder after what has become know as "The Great Escape".

ACKNOWLEDGMENTS

The information contained in "The Hampden File" has been gathered from four main sources; they are:

1. Personal Accounts from ex-aircrew who flew on Hampdens and from the "erks" who serviced them.

2. Official Records.

3. Squadron Historians, Ex-Service Organisations, Researchers in the United Kingdom.

4. Overseas Researchers.

1. Personal accounts from ex-Hampden personnel:

The assistance received from those whose accounts are used in the book is gratefully acknowledged as is that from others who made contact about the Hampdens. Their interest provided a continual source of encouragement during the compilation of "The Hampden File". The names are grouped in their different aircrew categories and squadrons, and where practicable an index number is given of the relevant incident. It is hoped that they will forgive the omission of details of rank and decorations, etc.

Pilots:

44 Sqn:	Dave Penman 5H3; Tony Reid 2C9; Mike Lewis.
49 Sqn:	Des Dunphy 3D6; Bob Hamer (AT112); Lewis Hodges 3D31
50 Sqn:	"Abdul" Abbott (AE251); Jimmy Bennett; "Weasel" Donaldson 2C15; George Potts 5B3; Chas Stenner; Gus Walker
61 Sqn:	Peter Tunstall 3D28; "Spooky" Barrett 3D13
83 Sqn:	Stan Harpham 2K9; Freddie Newall 5B11; Leonard Snaith 2C; Neil Svendsen 5B2; Tony Stamer; Rod Learoyd VC.
106 Sqn:	Vie Cooper (AE123); Wally Huggins; Chas Lockyer; Roy Haggar; Roger Purnell; Robert Wareing
144 Sqn:	Jimmy Bennett; Bob Galloway 2C2; Max Meyer; Bob Pearman 5A16; Colin Rawlins 2D11; Gordon Walters.
408 Sqn:	David Williams

31

415 Sqn:	Bill Adams 2J36; John Enns 2J37
420 Sqn:	Robert Kee 2D10
455 Sqn:	Grant Lindeman
A&AEE:	Tom Stanley

45 (Atlantic Transport) Group: Maurice Ratcliffe

Air Observers, Air Gunner Officers, Navigators

44 Sqn:	Andrew Coveyduck 3D8; Gerrie Harris (P2077); Alan Nicoll
50 Sqn:	John Day 2G; Gil Haworth 2D, 5G6; W J Johnstone (P1202); George Leonard (L4046)
83 Sqn:	Julian Badcock 5A52
144 Sqn:	W D Barrett 2J7; Dave Withey; "Timber" Woods 2K23; Vernon Smith
415 Sqn:	Jim Chapman; E.L.Rowe
455 Sqn:	Bob Anderson 2J7; Ray Lassiter (P1208)
32 OTU:	W N Switzer; P Moorhead Nav W/T.

Wireless Operator/Air Gunners and Air Gunners

44 Sqn:	Fred Ball; M Beale; Jim Taylor; Joe Dacey
49 Sqn:	Don Foster; **David Young 3D26**; John Fairbrother; "Chan" Chandler 5B10
50 Sqn:	Geoff Ashmore; Fred Bailey 2D8; Doug Barrie 2K26; Nairn "Robbie" Robertson 2G; Jim Mitchell; Bill Sykes
61 Sqn:	"Bernie" Bernard; Neil Prendergrast 2E2; Len Walker 3D2; John Brock 3D2
83 Sqn:	Eric Groves (L4057); Jack Lawrence-3D 10; Hector Macdonald
106 Sqn:	Tom Berry (AE123); Jim Palmer (AE123); Alien Wiseman; George Luke 3D23
144 Sqn:	Bert Earl* 2J13; Bernard Sowerby * 2J12; * Both groundcrew who flew on Russia flight; Jim Rowland, groundcrew on Russia detachment
408 Sqn:	Don Foster
415 Sqn:	Doug Stallard

420 Sqn:	David Semple
455 Sqn:	George Baynes; Bill McPhee; John McKissack, groundcrew on Russia detachment
489 Sqn:	Guy Gaskill 3D24; Eric Cameron

2. Official Records

Public Record Office at Kew

The Record Books of Squadrons Stations, Groups and Commands, and many files on particular aspects of Hampden operations were researched.

Air Historical Branch, London.

Permission was obtained to study Hampden "Crash" cards, "Movement" cards and "Contract" cards. The staff answered many written queries on Hampden fates.

RAF Museum, Hendon

The Museum photographic library proved to be a valuable source of photographs, and in the early stages of research Andrew Cormack offered advice and encouragement on the "Hampden File" project. The RAF Museum is continually adding to its Archive material and takes a keen interest in photographs of RAF aircraft, Log Books and general RAF memorabilia.

The Imperial War Museum, London

The staff of the photographic library assisted in the selection of suitable photographs.

The Commonwealth War Graves Commission, Maidenhead

War Cemetery Registers and the Runnymede Memorial Register provided information on crew fates. CWGC has to charge for Registers and queries on individual crew fates The service received proved well worth the financial outlay.

Public Archives of Canada, Ontario and the Supply and Services

Department, Ottawa proved to be valuable sources of good quality photographs. The courteous assistance given by the staff of all of the aforementioned Departments is acknowledged with gratitude.

Australian War Memorial, Canberra, answered several questions regarding aircraft and crew fates.

Bournemouth and Poole College of Art and Design

Sue Brown, a student at the Department of Technical Illustration, produced the cutaway drawing and several maps.

Air-Britain

Cliff Minney, the association's graphics adviser, produced the Hampden sideviews.

3. **Squadron Historians and Ex-service Associations and Researchers-in the United Kingdom**

Ron Low and Frank Harper of 83 Squadron; John Parley and Des Richards of 106 Squadron; Gus Dodson and Frank Priestly of 61 Squadron; Kenneth Green of 61 Squadron and Hemswell; Bob Cotterill and Bill Boorer of 144 Squadron; Alan White and Bert Dowty of 44 Squadron and Ray Leach of 50 Squadron. Peter Green provided various photographs and assisted with the reproduction of others. "Cee" Wadsworth provided photographs of 455 RAAF Squadron.

Ex-Service Organisations

Requests for information in newsletters of various ex-service organisations led to many Hampden contacts coming to light from The Aircrew Association, The Prisoner of War Association, the Royal Air Force Association, The Air Transport Auxiliary Association, The Handley Page Association, The Goldfish Club, The Air Sea Rescue/Marine Craft Club and the Lincolnshire Bomber Airfield Society. "FlyPast" and "Air-Britain Digest" were the two principal Aviation journals involved in seeking answers to particular problems.

Researchers in the United Kingdom

Brian Nicholls, who is engaged on the part – reconstruction of a Hampden at the Lincolnshire Aviation Heritage Centre at East Kirkby; Roy Nesbitt; Roger Hayward; Eric Thale; Mike Hodsman; Chaz Bowycr; John Foreman and Thomas E Willis who provided several interesting photographs, also corresponded.

Reproduced from 'The Hamden File'
by Harry Moyle (ISBN 0851301282)

Chapter 4

The Newspapers

Greenock Telegraph 18th May 1966

Modest RAF Hero's Five Prison Camp Escapes

How a 27-year-old Greenock RAF man came home on leave and told his parents of dangerous and hazardous prison escapes in Germany performed by his companions, when, in fact, he participated in the escapes, was told to a Telegraph reporter today.

The young man. Warrant Officer David Young, of 9 Brachelston Street, escaped from German prison camps five times, and for the daring exploits resulting from these escapes he has been awarded the Military Cross.

Mrs Young. David's mother, and Mrs Hodge, his sister, knew

35

absolutely nothing about the award until late last night. Although David Young has been home – on a month's leave – they never heard of his repeated attempts to escape during 4½ years' captivity. As late as March 1945, he risked recapture in Germany to take a sick RAF sergeant to hospital, but he never mentioned anything to his family.

David Young joined the RAF by chance. In the unsettled days of 1938 when pamphlets were being distributed about the three fighting Services. David thought that the Air Force suited him best.

"WEEK-END" FLYER

His mother, telling the story, said that although he was a week-end flyer he attended the Prestwick Flying School, and by the outbreak of war was fully able to take up duties with the RAF. He became a wireless operator and air gunner.

When he was last home, Mrs Hodge said. David looked none the worse for his experiences. "He was a little Nervous – but made light of everything, that was his way."

The officiai storv of David Young, who was educated at Greenock High School, is as follows:

September 1940 – Plane crashes near Courville, taken prisoner.

July 1941 – Escaped from prison camp near Berlin, recaptured.

September 1941 – "Free" for 2½ hours, recaptured.

June 1942 – Walked out of a camp with civilian workers, recaptured 25 miles away.

LIBERATED BY RUSSIANS

Three months later another escape. Recaptured near Baltic.

March, 1945. escaped while on the march.

Finally, on 4 May, the Greenock flyer was liberated by the victorious Russian armies.

At present he is in Preston undergoing an RAF refresher course. His wite, who comes from Stanford, is with him there, and he is expected home in a few days' time for "demob."

His father is chief steward on the MacBrayne steamer, Loch Fyne. Young himself was employed with the Gourock Rope Work Co., Port-Glasgow, before Joining the RAF.

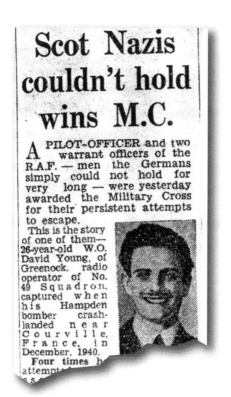

Scot Nazis couldn't hold wins M.C.

A PILOT-OFFICER and two warrant officers of the R.A.F. — men the Germans simply could not hold for very long — were yesterday awarded the Military Cross for their persistent attempts to escape. This is the story of one of them— 26-year-old W.O. David Young, of Greenock. radio operator of No. 49 Squadron, captured when his Hampden bomber crash-landed near Courville, France, in December, 1940.

Four times h attempt

SCOT NAZIS COULDN'T HOLD WINS M.C.

A PILOT-OFFICER and two warrant officers of the R.A.F. – men the Germans simply could not hold for very long – were yesterday awarded the Military Cross for their persistent attempts to escape. This is the story of one of them – 26-year-old W.O. David Young, of Greenock, radio operator of No. 49 Squadron, captured when his Hampden bomber crash-landed near Courville France in December, 1940.

Four times he attempted to escape and failed.

1 – Young and a colleague got clear by a tunnel;

2 – He broke away from a flour mill where he was working;

3 – Walked out of a camp with civilian workers:

4 – Hid under a cart.

Fifth time lucky for him – in March, 1945 – when he escaped by breaking away from a column of marching prisoners.

David Young is the son of Chief Steward Young of the M.V.

Lochfyne, and of Mrs Young, 9 Brachelston Street, Greenock.

Yesterday when a Scottish Daily Express reporter called at his home his father was at work, his mother on holiday, and first to get the news was his sister, Mrs. Hodge.

"All we knew," she said, "was that David had escaped, made his way to the Russian lines and was later picked up by British paratroopers."

Before the war, Young attended a flying school at the week-ends.

At the moment, he is on a refresher course at Preston.

GOOD NEWS FOR MOTHER
Son was Missing, Now Safe

A Greenock man. Sergeant David Young, of the R.A.F., who was reported missing early In December, is now officially stated to be a prisoner of war in Germany.

On the 7th of December, Mrs. Young, 9 Brachelston Street, mother of the airman who is only 21, received word from the War Office that her son was missing. Exactly one week later news came over the Wireless from Germany that David was in captivity.

This was very heartening, and on New Year's Eve came the official information that the airman was a prisoner of war.

Sergeant Young was a pupil of Greenock High School: Prior to the outbreak of war he was employed at the Gourock Ropework Company (Birkmyre) Office.

GREAT ESCAPER!

DAVID Young of Greenock holds the unusual honour of winning the Army's Military Cross during the war – although he was in the Royal Air Force!

David got the award after being shot down in his plane, escaping five times from the Germans and fighting his way into Berlin... in a Russian tank!

His girlfriend, Veronica, and family thought he had perished in 1940 when the 21-year-old wireless operator's Hampden bomber plunged in flames into a snow-covered French forest.

The navigator had forgotten his parachute, so the entire crew risked their necks to stay with the plane rather than leave him alone.

Fellow flyers who witnessed the crash went home to say there was no nope. But all of the crew survived the impact and ended up in harsh prisoner of war camps.

It was a couple of months before David's family learned he was alive. The news was sent via the airwaves by infamous Nazi propagandist, 'Lord Haw-Haw', whose venomous broadcasts from Berlin included the names of some prisoners of war.

It was heard by a family friend in Dempster Street who was so excited that she ran out half-dressed to nearby Brachelston Street to tell the Youngs that their son was still alive.

David was re-captured on the first four of his escapes, which involved various devious and dangerous flights from his captors.

It was fifth time lucky in March 1945 when he vanished from a long march of prisoners being taken east.

"I would have died from cold and starvation if I hadn't slipped away," he said.

He walked into a Russian tank regiment and was welcomed into the lead vehicle as it headed to the German capital.

He was handed over to the Americans, who took him to the Nazi concentration camp at Auschwitz in Poland to act as a witness to the atrocities.

"The corpses were lying there," David recalled. "It was terrible."

He came home to be re-united with Veronica, whom he married later that year. The couple have a son and daughter, two grandsons, two grand-daughters and a great-granddaughter.

David worked as wages office manager at Gourock Ropeworks and then in the time office at Scotts.

Looking back on the war, he said simply: "It was a long time ago."

SCOT'S FIVE ATTEMPTS TO ESCAPE
From Our Own Correspondent
LONDON GAZETTE 1946

The Military Cross has been awarded to a Scots airman Warrant Officer David Young, R.A.F.V.R., No 49 Squadron, who made four unsuccessful attempts to escape trom German prisoner of war camps during four and a half years of captivity. After escaping at his fifth attempt he was liberated by the Russians.

He was born in 1919 at Greenock, where his home still is, and joined the R.A.F. in March 1939.

Warrant Officer Young was the wireless operator of a Hampden aircraft that crash-landed near Courville in December 1940. The crew were taken to Dulag Luft at Frankfurt, and transferred to Stalag Luft I. at Barth in March, 1941

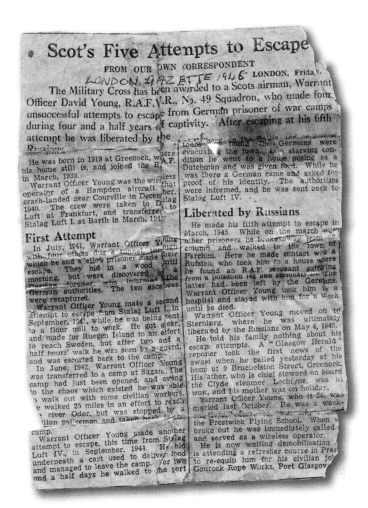

Scot's Five Attenpts to Escape

FROM OUR OWN CORRESPONDENT

LONDON GAZETTE 1946 LONDON, Friday.

The Military Cross has been awarded to a Scots airman, Warrant Officer David Young, R.A.F.V.R., No. 49 Squadron, who made four unsuccessful attempts to escape from German prisoner of war camps during four and a half years of captivity. After escaping at his fifth attempt he was liberated by the Russians.

He was born in 1919 at Greenock, where his home still is, and joined the R.A.F. in March, 1939.

Warrant Officer Young was the wireless operator of a Hampden aircraft that crash-landed near Courville in December, 1940. The crew were taken to Dulag Luft at Frankfurt, and transferred to Stalag Luft I. at Barth in March, 1941.

First Attempt

In July, 1941, Warrant Officer Young, with four others dug a tunnel, through which he and a fellow prisoner made their escape. They hid in a wood until morning, but were discovered by a German forester, who informed the German authorities. The two escapees were recaptured.

Warrant Officer Young made a second attempt to escape from Stalag Luft I. in September, 1941, while he was being sent to a flour mill to work. He got clear, and made for Ruegen Island in an effort to reach Sweden, but after two and a half hours' walk he was seen by a guard, and was escorted back to the camp.

In June, 1942, Warrant Officer Young was transferred to a camp at Sagan. The camp had just been opened, and owing to the chaos which existed he was able to walk out with some civilian workers. He walked 25 miles in an effort to reach river Oder, but was stopped by a Italian policeman and taken back to camp.

Warrant Officer Young made another attempt to escape, this time from Stalag Luft IV., in September, 1944. He hid underneath a cart used to deliver food and managed to leave the camp. For two and a half days he walked to the port

there, young Germans were evacuating the town, in a starving condition he went to a house posing as a Dutchman and was given food. While he was there a German came and asked for proof of his identity. The authorities were informed, and he was sent back to Stalag Luft IV.

Liberated by Russians

He made his fifth attempt to escape in March, 1945. While on the march with other prisoners he broke away from the column and walked to the town of Parchim. Here he made contact with a Russian, who took him to a house where he found an R.A.F. sergeant suffering from a poisoned leg and seriously ill. The latter had been left by the Germans. Warrant Officer Young took him to a hospital and stayed with him for a week until he died.

Warrant Officer Young moved on to Sternberg, where he was ultimately liberated by the Russians on May 4, 1945.

He told his family nothing about his escape attempts. A "Glasgow Herald" reporter took the first news of the award when he called yesterday at his home at 9 Brachelston Street, Greenock. His father, who is chief steward on board the Clyde steamer Lochfyne, was at work, and his mother was on holiday.

Warrant Officer Young, who is 26, was married last October. He was a week before the war at the Prestwick Flying School. When war broke out he was immediately called and served as a wireless operator.

He is now waiting demobilisation, is attending a refresher course in Prestwick to re-equip him for his civilian job at Gourock Rope Works, Port Glasgow.

First Attempt

In July 1941 Warrant Officer Young with four others dug a tunnel, through which he and a fellow prisoner made their escape. They hid in a wood until morning, but were discovered by a German forester, who informed the German authorities. The two escapees were recaptured.

Warrant Officer Young made a second attempt to escape from Stalag Luft I. in September, 1941, while he was being sent to a flour mill to work. He got clear and made for Ruegen Island in an effort to reach Sweden, but after two and a half hours' walk he was seen by a guard and was escorted back to the camp.

In June, 1942. Warrant Officer Young was transferred to a camp at Sagan. The camp had just been opened, and owing the chaos which existed he was able to walk out with some civilian workers. He walked 25 miles in an effort to reach the river Oder, but was stopped by a civilian policeman and taken back to the camp.

Warrant Officer Voung made anolher attempt to escape, this time from Stalag Luft IV., in September, 1944. He hid underneath a cart used to deliver food and managed to leave the camp. For two and a half days he walked to the port of Kinsberg on the Baltic and on arriving there he found the Germans were evacuating the town. In a starving condition he went to a house posing as a Dutchman and was given food. While he was there a German came and asked for proof of his identity. The authorities were informed and he was sent back to Stalag Luft IV.

Liberated by Russians

He made his fifth attempt to escape in March 1945. While on the march with other prisoners he broke away from the column and walked to the town of Parchim. Here he made contact with a Russian, who took him to a house where he found an R.A.F. sergeant suffering from a poisoned leg and seriously ill. The latter had been left by the Germans. Warrant Officer Young took him to a hospital and stayed with him for a week until he died.

Warrant Officer Young moved on to Sternberg, where he was ultimately liberated by the Russians on May 4, 1945.

He told his family nothing about his escape attempts. A 'Glasgow Herald' reporter took the first news of his award when he called yesterday at his home at 9 Brachelston Street, Greenock. His father, who is chief steward on board the Clyde steamer Lochfyne, was at work, and his mother was on holiday.

Warrant Officer Young, who is 26, was married last October. He was a week-end flyer before the war and attended the Prestwick Flying School. When war broke out he was immediately called up and served as a wireless operator.

He is now waiting demobilisation and is attending a refresher course in Prestwick to re-equip him for his civilian job at Gourock Rope Works, Port Glasgow.

" . . . . . . F/O David Young, M.C., R.A.F.

Photo.—R. Love.

It was an odd tale that I heard last week-end while chatting to Flying Officer David Young, Adjutant of the Air Training Corps Company at Greenock, which has many Port boys in its ranks.

F/O Young occupies an executive position at the Gourock Rope Works, so although he lives in Greenock his ties with Port Glasgow are very strong. His story once again proves: that truth's more strange than fiction.

A youthful looking 38, I was first intrigued by the decorative which he wore on his tunic. I recognised the conventional medal ribbon, but what

on earth was an Air Force Officer doing with that exclusively coveted military award,' the M.C.?

And thereby hangs a tale. Modestly and diffidently, Mr Young told me his story. Twenty years ago he was in the R.N.V.R., and was on flying duties almost as soon as war broke out.

At the end of 1940 while engaged in operational duties over Germany, he was shot down and for four and a half years vanished into the hell of a German Offlag, near Lubeck, one of the famed cities of the Hanseatic League of Medieval days.

There he soon joined an escapers club with Wing-Commander Douglas Bader, and other air aces, but it wasn't to give his captors the slip and made his way across East Prussia into Russian occupied territory, where he joined up with the spearheads of the Russian Armies which were closing in on Berlin.

There, attached to the Soviet Forces, he trained Russky soldiers and airmen in signalling and navigational duties—in fact anything to which he could turn a hand.

I asked Flying Officer Young

how he came by the Military Cross.

It still was a mystery to him he told me "I have yet to hear of any other Scottish Officer in the R.A.F., who got the award." The R.A.F. equivalent is, of course, the D.F.C.

Mr Young surmises that the Russians who probably made the recommendation automatically assumed that every officer they captured was a soldier in the British Army.

This gallant officer, who now devotes all his spare time to A.T.C. activities is rightly proud of his enique decoration which he carries with so much distinction.

GREENOCK TELEGRAPH

It was an odd tale that I heard last week-end while chatting to Flying Officer David Young, Adjutant of the Air Training Corps Company at Greenock, which has many Port boys in its ranks.

F/O Young occupies an executive position at the Gourock Rope Works, so although he lives in Greenock his ties with Port Glasgow are very strong. His story once again proves that truth's more strange than fiction.

A youthful looking 38, I was first intrigued by the decorative which he wore on his tunic. I recognised the conventional medal ribbon, but what on earth was an Air Force Officer doing with that exclusively coveted military award, the M.C.?

And thereby hangs a tale. Modestly and diffidently, Mr Young told me his story. Twenty years ago he was in the R.N.V.R., and was on flying duties almost as soon as war broke out.

At the end of 1940 while engaged in operational duties over Germany, he was shot down and for four and a half years vanished into the hell of a German Offlag, near Lubeck, one of the famed cities of the Hanseatic League of Medieval days.

There he soon joined an escapers club with Wing-Commander Douglas Bader, and other air aces, but it wasn't until 1945 that he managed to give his captors the slip and made his way across East Prussia into Russian occupied territory, where he joined up with the spearheads of the Russian Armies which were closing in on Berlin.

There, attached to the Soviet Forces, he trained Russky soldiers and airmen in signalling and navigational duties – in fact anything to which he, could turn a hand

I asked Flying Officer Young how he came by the Military Cross.

It still was a mystery to him he told me "I have yet to hear of any other Scottish Officer in the R.A.F., who got the award." The R.A.F. equivalent is, of course, the D.F.C.

Mr Young surmises that the Russians who probably made the recommendation automatically assumed that every officer they captured was a soldier in the British Army.

This gallant officer, who now devotes all his spare time to A.T.C. activities is rightly proud of his unique decoration which he carries with so much distinction.

Publisher's note:

The preceding texts are reproduced directly as the newspapers had printed them.

Chapter 5

Air Training Corps

The publishers are grateful to Duncan McKinnon for the following information on David's involvement with the Air Training Corps and RAF clubs in the Greenock area. In addition, Duncan's information on the formation of the ATC and the 49f Squadron, including his own services as CO adds greatly to the history. G.M.

From Duncan McKinnon:

David Young – Pre War

In relation to David's Air Training Corps history, I gained some valuable information from Mr Alex Dorrain, the last known holder of the Lady MacRoberts 'MacRoberts Reply' lapel badge which she awarded to him at her home in Aberdeen. Alex is certain that David Young served with him as a 49f Sqn cadet in its formative years before going on to serve in the Royal Air Force.

The following is an interesting note from the 49f Squadron's history file – Prior to the formation of the ATC, Mr Hector Russell ran a youth athletic club locally. When the ATC was initially formed, it consisted of fifty Squadrons, hence the (f) denoting a founder Squadron. Hector Russell promptly enrolled his club en masse into the ATC and just made it to become the 49th founder Squadron. In those early years the primary function of the ATC was to train young men for Royal Air Force and war time service.

David Young – Post War

As mentioned before, information sources are now very limited and, as I have said myself, David's quiet and reserved nature has left a very thin paper trail, making it difficult to get a clear picture of his post war life.

With regard to his RAFVR(T)/ATC service, I am able to say with confidence that David was indeed an RAFVR(T) Officer and that he did command 49f (Greenock) 'MacRoberts Reply' Squadron, Air Training Corps.

Confirmation of this comes from Mrs Margaret Wooler, another RAFA member. Margaret and her late husband Alistair were long standing social friends of David and Veronica. Margaret report's that Alistair joined 49f Squadron in 1950 as a lad of 14yrs, and that David Young was the Officer Commanding* throughout his cadet service, until he was called up for national service in 1955 when Alistair served in the RAF Regiment.

David and Veronica were popular amongst their RAFA and RAF Club friends, and attended most Saturday dances and special events. Although David was a life member of both RAFA and Club, most of those consulted concluded that David was generally 'a quiet man who kept himself to himself.'

After completing his National Service, Alistair and Margaret Wooler became Club members. They soon struck up a friendship with David and Veronica which was to become lifelong and David would always refer to Alistair as 'My boy.' Margaret reports that David could be quite humorous on nights out and, although from time to time over drinks friends would try to glean some insight into his service experiences, he was reluctant to go too deep and light heartedly change the subject.

Over the later years David maintained an interest in 49f Squadron and in the late 70's donated a silver trophy to the squadron. He would frequently enquire how the squadron was getting along.

A further chat with Margaret confirms that David did indeed encourage Alistair in his post-national service contributions to the ATC, RAFA, and the RAF Club. She also remembers working beside David at Gourock Ropeworks in Port Glasgow in the 60's.

During David's time as Squadron Commander, cadet training was geared more towards service entry than it is today. At the old Greenock Squadron HQ there was a small workshop where hands on training in electrical, mechanical, and engineering were taught. In this capacity, David's own knowledge and skills would have come fully into play. Of equal importance, just as it is today, Squadron Commanders would

AIR TRAINING CORPS

This Certificate

expresses my appreciation of the services given to the Air Training Corps

by ___Flying Officer D. Young, M.C.___

while serving from __20th May, 1953__ *to* __5th November, 1959__ *in the*

Training Branch of the Royal Air Force Volunteer Reserve.

AIR MINISTRY.

31st December, 1959

D. A. Boyle M.R.A.F.

CHIEF OF THE AIR STAFF.

David Young's ATC service certificate signed by Sir Dermot Boyle, Chief of The Air Staff.

endeavour to help cadets develop and expand their skills, build confidence, encourage participation, instil pride, and develop good citizenship. Outside official duties, through a network of friends and local business associates, 49f Sqn Commanders traditionally do all they can to place cadets in employment whilst (quietly) ensuring that disadvantaged cadets would not be excluded from opportunities.

The squadron is proud that over the years many of its cadets have gone on to excel in life, e.g. Sir Albert McQuarrie (Industry captain), Sir Simpson Stevenson (Ex Town Provost and Chairman of Argyll and Clyde Health Board), a current Air Vice Marshal, a senior SAS Officer, an RAFVR(T) Wing Commander, Several ATC Squadron Commanders and thousands of others who became good honest hard working adults.

My own service career took me to RAF bases throughout Britain, the Middle East, Kenya, Malta and Holland. I must not neglect to give credit to the many wise and experienced service personnel who inspired, motivated and advised me through the years. I especially recall David Young being an important one of those.

I met David for the first time in 1963 at the RAF Club in Greenock. I was on embarkation leave prior to being posted to Aden and had made a weekend social visit to the club. Whilst at the bar, David struck up a conversation, obviously interested to find out more about this young uniformed visitor to his club. I explained my imminent posting abroad and my apprehension that this was a developing trouble spot. As the evening came to a close, David came from his table to wish me bon-voyage saying, 'Go and do your best, you will find satisfaction knowing you have done your best.'

After regular service I brought all of my RAF knowledge and skills back to the local Air Training Corps. On becoming a squadron commander in 1984, 1 continued the OC responsibilities as I described in David's service section. I retired from RAFVR(T) service in 2003, having been granted six years of extended service beyond the normal retirement age of 55 years, and with 19 years as OC became the longest serving OC in 49f Squadron history.

On reflection, did I make the right decision as a young man in 1961? You bet I did... Did I do my best? Well my collection of

Meritorious Service Commendations would suggest that I did.

And yes, I did find the satisfaction that David Young had spoken about many years ago.

Publisher's note:

*As the book was being prepared, Alan and Pat rediscovered the Certificate of Service (illustrated in this chapter) that was presented to David Young by the then RAF Chief of Staff, Marshal of the Royal Air Force Sir Dermot Boyle in 1959. This positively identifies David's service with the 49f Squadron.

Postscript

In 1945 our parents decided to move north to my father's home town of Greenock. My father returned to the company that he worked for pre war, and my mother settled into her new surroundings.

David and Veronica went on to lead a happy life having lots of grandchildren and great grandchildren.

In 1963 while driving home from Glasgow they were involved in a head on collision with another vehicle (my father actually being given his last rites at the scene), and were both seriously injured. But again, as in the past, their spirit, love, and determination pulled them through.

My father worked in shipbuilding until the early 1980s, when unfortunately there was a general decline in the Scottish shipbuilding industry and he retired in 1981.

They lived a long and happy life together, our mother working until she was 72 as a director of a company, and enjoyed many holidays in Spain (Nerja), where they made many friends.

Sadly in 2007 our father passed away in the Erskine Ex serviceman's hospital, and two years later on the exact date (29th June) our mother joined him.

Alan Young and Pat Young McEwan
December 2011.